POETRY EUROPE
Europoésie

First published in 2009 by
Dedalus Press
13 Moyclare Road
Baldoyle
Dublin 13
Ireland

www.dedaluspress.com

Poetry Europe / *Europoésie* editorial address:
European Academy of Poetry
24, The Heath
Cypress Downs
Dublin 6W
Ireland
—*or*—
4 rue Comte de Ferraris
L 1518 Luxembourg

www.poetryeurope.com

ISBN 978 1 906614 10 2

Typesetting by Sarah Baldwin
Cover image © Lisa Valder/iStockphoto.com

'Poetry Europe / *Europoésie*'
receives financial assistance
from the Arts Council

Poetry Europe
Europoésie

Edited by
JOHN F. DEANE

Dedalus Press

L'Académie Européenne de poésie a pour but principal d'assurer la place du poème dans la presse, à la radio et à la télévision de tous les pays d'Europe, place aujourd'hui minime ou contestée. Elle considère de son devoir de défendre cette activité artistique, qui contribue à définir la sensibilité et l'identité du continent. Outre ces réunions de travail, un programme sera élaboré: lectures publiques, discussions et débats avec les enseignants, entretiens avec les media, en particulier à Luxembourg et à Mersch mais partout où cela sera possible et nécessaire. L'association a pour objet de soigner les relations et contacts nationaux et internationaux entre gens de lettres, d'éditer des journaux, des livres ou autres publications. Elle pourra accomplir toutes opérations généralement quelconques, entreprendre toutes démarches nécessaires et prendre toutes mesures se rattachant directement ou indirectement à la réalisation de son objet social.

The European Academy of Poetry was founded in Luxembourg on 31st March 1996 by Alain Bosquet, Philippe Jones and Anise Koltz. Its full complement of permanent members will be thirty and the Academy is in the process of electing thirty correspondent, or associate, members, the majority of whom will be drawn from those countries not yet represented in the Academy. The Academy will ultimately consist of 30 permanent members and 30 correspondents. The headquarters is located in Maison Servais, Mersch, Luxembourg, in the National Centre of Literature. The principal aim of the Academy is to ensure the place of the poem in newspapers, radio and television throughout all the countries of Europe. The Academy considers it its duty to defend this artistic activity which contributes to the definition of the sensibility and the identity of the continent. As well as its working sessions it will develop a programme of public readings, discussions and debates, with teachers, with the media, especially in Luxembourg but also everywhere such action is required.

CONTENTS

EUROPEAN
ACADEMY
OF POETRY

A SELECTION OF CONTEMPORARY IRISH POETS

ESSAYS

Alain Bosquet

Alain Bosquet was born in Odessa in 1919 and died in Paris in 1998. He published many collections of verse and was well known as a critic, novelist and essayist. He leaves a widow, Norma, currently living in Paris, and patron of the Academy which was founded by Alain Bosquet, in Luxembourg, in 1996.

from **"Le tourment de Dieu"**

«Je ne suis pas Dieu». dit Dieu,
«qu'à cause du mot dieu,
auquel je rends hommage.
Je lui promets, pour mieux le mériter,
d'offrit à l'univers
la force et la musique,
la fable et le bonheur.»
«Je ne suis Dieu», dit Dieu,
«que pour montrer l'exemple,
mais un seul mot est bien trop faible.
Je cherche un synonyme.»

• • •

Dieu dit: «Entre moi-même et moi,
je sens qu'il manque
une manière de douceur;
c'est pourquoi j'improvise
un colibri, quelque rosée,
une île très légère,
un chant d'amour, un songe intermittent
où se promène un autre dieu.»

• • •

Dieu que nous bénissons.
Donne-nous, s'il te plait, l'enfant
et le blé qui s'agitent,
Dieu qui es le seul dieu.
Prête-nous, pour ta gloire,
la certitude et la clarté,
Dieu que nous imitons.
Mais Dieu murmure:
«L'amour ne suffit pas,
et la prière est un mensonge:
soyez vous-mêmes
des dieux.»

• • •

J'ai présidé le concile des dieux,
disant à l'un:
"Prends soin de l'horizon, il souffre";
à l'autre:
"Trouve à l'étoile un domicile fixe";
au troisième: "Remets de l'ordre dans le temps
car l'hiver cherche noise à tes autres saisons";
au quatrième:
"Fais un effort pour mieux comprendre le cheval,
le feu, le fleuve et l'océan."
J'ai donné la parole à tous les dieux,
qui pourtant se sont tus.
Je dois améliorer mon âme

"I'm only God", says God,
"by reason of the word god,
to which I pay due homage.
I promise, so that I become more worthy of it,
to offer to the universe
strength and music,
fable and hapiness."
"I'm only God", says God,
"to show example,
though one single word is far too weak.
I'm searching for a synonym."

• • •

God says: "Between me and myself
I sense that there is missing
a sort of sweetness;
and that is why I improvise
a humming bird, some dew,
a gentle island,
a love song, a periodic dream
in which another god is walking."

• • •

God whom we bless.
Grant to us, please, the child
and the restless wheat.
God who is alone god.
Lend to us, for your own glory,
certainty and clarity,
God whom we imitate.
But God only murmurs:
"Love is not enough,
and prayer is but a lie;
be yourselves
gods."

• • •

I chaired the council of the gods,
saying to the first one:
"Take care, you, of the horizon, it is suffering",
and to another:
"Find a permanent home for the star";
to a third: "Put order back into time
for winter is quarrelling with your other seasons;"
and to the fourth:
"Make an effort to understand the horse a little better,
the fire too, the river and the ocean."
I offered the floor to all the gods,
but they all remained silent.
I shall have to improve my soul.

Translated by John F. Deane

Fiona Sampson

Fiona has published fourteen books — including poetry, philosophy of language and studies of writing process. The most recent are *The Distance Between Us* (Seren, 2005) and *Writing: Self and Reflexivity* (with Celia Hunt; Macmillan, 2005).

In 2008 Carcanet publisher her collection *Common Prayer*, which was short-listed for the T.S. Eliot Prize. Her translations include Jaan Kaplinski, an anthology of younger Central European poets, and *Orient Express*, of which she was founding editor.

She is the editor of *Poetry Review*.

Autumn in Clun

You came: we saw: we heard:
.... word.
     - On a bench at Clun

A breeze disturbs leaves
which articulate what moves on
                    and away

to be a premonition of change,
or remembered emotion,

so long ago
      that you mistrust the memory.

And again –
its cool draft on your skin

like a ghost,
stirring the leaves with breath

which passes across your lips
in a sigh –

was this what they saw?

Out picking horse mushrooms
in a dewy quiff of grass,

or walking the dog
below the brim of woods:

did they see gold
move between elder twigs,

assume the form of a man
who walked along with them a way –

talking about the weather
in the decent way of country neighbours,

or seeming to listen
as if to echoes
                in a wide vale of meaning –

then vanished?

The miraculous stone
waits at the curb,

a dressed ingot.
Here are the blue votive flowers,

the bench with its unremarkable view
of town and farms,

the everyday movement of light
across fields rising in parallels from the river –

gold, pink, grey –
They're grave-cloths.

Doxology

God crush
this stem of anger
God crumple my neck
like paper

Lord of envy –
Vinegar King –
refuse me
your unceasing heaven

Let me sleep
hopeless and whole
attended
by each nightly ghost

and wake at last
in borrowed skin
to clothe the shame
that Love let in –

You whose daylight
thrills the nerves –
burn me
as I deserve

Ana Blandiana

Ana Blandiana was born in Timisoara, Romania, in 1942.
She is a freelance writer and probably the most widely
celebrated contemporary Romanian poet.

English versions are signed by Peter Jay and Anca
Cristofovici. French versions by Luiza Palanciuc.

Non option

Au grand jugement appelée,
Celui qui finit par le renvoi sur terre,
Moi, non coupable ayant été déclarée,
J'ai reçu le droit
De me choisir moi-même.
Ni homme, ni femme,
Ni un quelconque animal je n'ai voulu être,
Ni oiseau, ni plante.
On entend les secondes tomber
De l'immense droit de choisir
On les entend cogner sur la pierre:
Non, non, non, non.
En vain traînée devant le jugement,
En vain non coupable.

Non-Choice

Brought to that great judgement
That ends with the sending to earth,
I, found innocent,
Have been given the right
To choose myself.
But neither man, nor woman,
Nor an animal did I want to be,
Nor a bird, or plant.
The seconds are heard dropping
From the great right to choose,
They are heard breaking against rock:
No, no, no, no.
In vain brought to the judgement,
In vain innocent.

Condition

Je suis
telle
un petit grain dans le sablier
qui
ne peut devenir temps
que
lorsqu'il
tombe.

Condition

I
am like
sand in the hourglass
which
can be time
only
in
falling.

Habit

Parfois le matin
Je me réveille glacée
Et encore à moitié endormie
Je tire, engourdie et transie, sur moi
Mon jeune corps,
Chaud, soyeux,
Dans lequel je me réfugie
En claquant des dents tel un enfant,
Heureuse qu'un autre jour,
Un jour entier
Je serai
À l'abri de l'éternité.

Vestment

Sometimes in the morning
I wake up frozen
And, still half asleep,
I pull, drowsy and shivering,
My yang, warm, silky
Body over myself.
I wrap myself in it
Teeth chattering childishly,
Happy that for one more day,
One whole day
I will be
In a shelter from eternity.

Knut Ødegård

Knut is one of the most widely translated contemporary poets writing in Norway. He has published many collections of his poetry, most recently a collected poems. He commutes between Iceland and Norway and is founder and honorary president of the international literary Bjornson Festival held in Molde, Norway.

Vinner Som Ekspederer I Butikk

Det er ein slik kald
og klår dag i desember: Ny-
månen skin som ein glinsande buk over kvinnene
som ekspederer i butikk, dei er
på veg i dette skìnet til jobb. Det er tidleg
morgon no, og i denne glidande rørsla av kvinner
i det gulgråe skìnet i snøen er òg ho som ekspederer
i urmakarbutikken.

Eg har dikta denne kvinna
som pustar ni timar kvar dag blant alle desse urverka
desse tikkande klokkene og pendlane som fyk ikring:
Det er slikt eit ustabilt vêr, slike bråe
skiftingar, omslag, i nedbør
og temperatur. Det byrjar snø stilt no i diktet
der ho låser seg inn i butikken i Storgata.
Eg kallar henne Lisbet.

Alt er her, tenkjer ho, Lisbet
som ekspederer i butikk: Alt
som finst er her. Ko-ko
seier gaukuret på veggen
når urmakaren kjem inn

og ho kan gå ut for ein morgonrøyk.
Eg diktar dei andre kvinnene som ekspederer
i butikk koma ut med dei svartglinsande veskene sine
på same tid som Lisbet: Dei er litt tjukke
og sexy og dei opnar dei glatte veskene sine, fingrane
med svartlakkerte negler leitar etter røykpakka og
lighteren. Vêret så ustabilt

slår om, blir råare no, der dei står ute og røyker, held
sigarettane sine med desse silkemjuke struttande fingrane
med svart lakkerte negler. Det er regn
i vente. Våte
sigarettar, menthol, med avtrykk
av sjokkrosa leppestift på filteret.

Ja alt er her, tenkjer Lisbet
som går inn i urmakarbutikken
frå sneipen som ulmar på fortauet: Alt
er.
Ko-ko, seier gaukuret.
Ko-ko.

Det er urverk dregne opp
overalt der lungene hennar
pustar, det er hennar
jobb å ekspd. her: Vi nærmar oss jul og det ligg kram snø
som smeltar mot kvelden der trafikken
med sine pigghjul bryt is over den mørke
materien, i Storgata går Lisbet
i raude skinnstøvleggar i sørpa,
heim.

Den mørke materien siv ut i det kvite
som eit mønster eit framandt språk, tenkjer ho,
der støvletthælane hennar
skjer seg inn dit, i det svarte underdjupet.

Women who serve in shops

It is one of those cold
and clear days in December: the new
moon shines like a gleaming belly over the women
who serve in shops, they are
on their way in this shining to their jobs. It is early
morning now, and in this gliding movement of women
in the yellow-gray shining in the snow is also the one who serves
in the watchmaker's shop.

I have invented this woman
who breathes nine hours each day among all these timepieces
these ticking clocks and pendulums that fly around:
It is such unstable weather, such sudden
changes, reversals, in precipitation
and temperature. Now it begins to snow silently in the poem
as she unlocks the door of the shop in the High Street.
I call her Lisbet.

Everything is here, she thinks, Lisbet
who serves in the shop: Everything
that exists is here. Cuckoo
says the clock on the wall
when the watchmaker comes in

and she can go out for a morning smoke.
I invent the other women who serve
in shops: they come out with their shiny black handbags
at the same time as Lisbet: They are slightly plump
and sexy and they open their smooth handbags, the fingers
with black lacquered nails grope for cigarette packets and
the lighter. The weather, so unstable,

changes, becomes rawer now as they stand outside smoking, holding
their cigarettes with these silk-smooth bulging fingers
with black lacquered nails. Rain is
on the way. Wet
cigarettes, menthol, with prints
of shocking pink lipstick on the filter.

Yes, everything is here, Lisbet thinks
as she leaves the butt glowing on the pavement
and enters the watchmaker's shop: Everything
is.
Cuckoo, says the clock.
Cuckoo.

There are clocks drawn up
everywhere her lungs
breathe, it is her
job to serve here: It's nearly Christmas and sticky snow lies
melting towards evening where the traffic
with its studded tyres breaks the ice over the dark
matter, in the High Street Lisbet walks
in red leather boots in the slush,
home.

The dark matter seeps out into the white
like a pattern in a foreign language, she thinks,
where the heels of her boots
cut into the black depths under her feet.

Translated by Brian McNeill

Philippe Jones

Born in Brussels, poet and novelist as well as an art historian. He was director of the Musée des Beaux-Arts from 1961 to 1984. He is a founder and life member of the European Academy of Poetry and has published many collections.

His awards include the prize of the French Academy.

Source mémorable

Un souvenir accueille et le sombre et le feu

la glace est poids et transparence
un corps se rêve un mur se fige

oiseau diras-tu l'heure

Une feuille qui bouge évoque une figure

vent es-tu forme ou vide

et de moraine et de mémoire
naissent du jeu les devenirs

Un signe obscur ou sourd précède l'écriture

Memorable Spring

A memory welcomes both darkness and fire

ice is weight and transparency
a body dreams itself a wall stiffens

bird will you tell the time

A leaf moving evokes a shape

wind are you form or void

from both moraine and memory
are born the destinies of the game

An obscure or a dumb sign obscures writing

Translated by John F. Deane

István Turczi

István Turczi is a native of the northern small town of Tata.
He worked at a number of odd jobs after graduating from
high school, from night doorman to chauffeur, eventually
gaining admission to the University of Budapest from
which he graduated in 1983 with a diploma in Hungarian,
English and Finno-Ugric Languages and Literature.
Subsequently he worked in the Ministry of Culture and
Education before turning to freelance writing in 1988.
István and Anna Palos Turczi run the publishing house
Parnasszus, producing a quarterly magazine and books
by contemporary poets, translators and essayists.

Friendship

I'm scared.
Ever since the trees entered my room to warm up,
it's been a tight squeeze.
Suspiciously they blinked at me: just what kind
of creature am I?
Why all the legs, hands, why the gleaming
eyes? And why isn't my hair green?
They tasted my dinner, pulled up their noses,
flicked through my books, took pity on me.
The bed gave them a cramp in their hips, while
the postman's motorbike scared them to death.
They came to like Mozart though. Each afternoon
the cheery sound of the flute welcomed me home.
Till the blossoming buds did our friendship last.
This morning the lumberjack arrived,
and by means of a greeting he cut
a nice part out of my past.
The trees clung together.

Edoardo Sanguineti

Edoardo Sanguineti was born in Italy in 1930 and has been professor of Italian Literature in Genoa. As one of the most important poets of the neo-vanguard movement he has been innovative, exciting and challenging. He has writen plays and many of his poems have been set to music by Luciano Berio. He has published several collections of his poetry and been translated into many languages.

D.F. 99

il 16 agosto è un lunedì (e il calcolo delle ore
è una follia francofortese : e vedi, l'agenda non è chiara) :
nessuno (pare) apprezza in volo, qui, questo champán :
e chi ha detto (forse l'ha detto Ese : ma forse io
medesimo) : " perché leggere un altro libro è una follia
ecc. "? (se questa fu una domanda, non lo so : ricordo
niente) :

        è sera tarda, poi : e noi siamo all'Hotel Prom,
nella famosa (e infame : e (semi) "apocalittica") zona
rosa (Versailles 46) :

        alla Cantina La Opera, si narra
(si vede), sul soffitto, c'è un foro di pallottola
(firmato Pancho Villa) :

        (didascalia : nove anni dopo) :
mi arriva la cartolina con qualche Zapata (con sus
esposas, en Morelos, foto Hugh Brehme, c. 1910) :

D.F. 99

august 16 is a monday (calculating exact time
is frankfurtian folly: anyway, the diary is unclear) :
nobody on the flight (it seems) appreciated the champagne:
and who said (maybe Ese, maybe
myself) : "reading another book is foolish
etc."? (was it framed as a question? I don't know: I remember
nothing) :
        it is now late evening and we are at the Hotel Prom,
in the famous (and infamous: and (semi) "apocalyptic") pink
zone (Versailles 46) :
            at the Cantina La Opera, one reads
(one sees) on the ceiling, there is a shooting gallery
(signed Pancho Villa) :
            (caption: nine years later) :
a card comes to me showing some Zapata (with his
exhibits, in Morelos, photo Hugh Brehme, c. 1910)

Translated by Pádraig J. Daly

Michael Schmidt

Michael Schmidt was born in Mexico in 1947. He studied at Harvard and at Wadham College, Oxford. He is currently Professor of Poetry at Glasgow University, where he is convenor of the Creative Writing M.Litt programme.

He is a founder (1969) and editorial and managing director of Carcanet Press Limited, and a founder (1972) and general editor of *PN Review*. A Fellow of the Royal Society of Literature, he received an O.B.E. in 2006 for services to poetry. His latest collection of poetry is *The Resurrection of the Body*.

Herr Schnabel

'Rudolf Schnabel was sitting outside his little house, a carpenter, retired,
and had his dwarf there too.' Letter from E.S., 16 August 2007

Herr Schnabel is sitting out in the sun. His dwarf
Plays in the shade, pulls geranium heads.
It's hot in a calm way. Hot. 'Now he's grown up
He can still fit the clothes he wore as a boy, the shoes
Only have had to get bigger, see how big his feet.
He sleeps in the cot I built for when he was five'
(Herr Schnabel was a carpenter before)
'In the pointy space there up under the gable.
And he makes himself useful, you see how he keeps busy.'
We watch him, rooting now deep in the shrubbery.
'He sometimes whistles. I don't like him to sing.
Though he is little he has a grown-up voice
Like a toad, ugly, gruff. Come, Kugel, whistle.'
He emerges into the sun and stands quite still.
He tilts his head to one side, makes a bristled beak,
Emits a fluty dance tune, tapping a foot.
Herr Schnabel pats his crown, 'Enough,' he says,
Resting a hand on the hump of this pet of his.

Above our heads, a cat projects its yellow paws
Over the edge of the gutter. It yawns like an angel,
All its needles sharp and clean, then recomposes,
Golden, unwinged, a purring emanation.
Kugel meanwhile takes the besom and sweeps up the heads,
Whistling a little, growling a little, sweeping.
'When I am gone who will look after Kugel.'
Herr Schnabel concentrates on the river, beyond,
The trees in sunlight climbing to the crest
And behind, another crest and beyond that
A stark escarpment, and the spinning sun.

I don't dare ask if he has other children.
I don't dare ask if Kugel is his son.
He says to Kugel, 'Bring two glasses, the schnaps,
The speck, and a black loaf. Be quick now.'

John F. Deane

Born Achill Island, 1943, founder of Poetry Ireland and
The Poetry Ireland Review. Member of Aosdána, winner
of the O'Shaughnessy Award, the Marten Toonder Award
and others; latest collection of poetry *A Little Book of
Hours*, (Carcanet 2008).

Nightwatch

In our suburban villages, our dormitory towns
we lie secure. But at the city's core
up and down the crack-tiled steps of the men's
shelter, they pass who could be minister

or president or priest – but are not;
in dust-striped suits and mismatched waistcoats
who could be civil servants – but are not;
greased and creased and ill-at-ease they ghost,

side-staggering, our streets, who might
be Plato, Luther, Hopkins but for some tiny thing
that slipped and shifted them a little to the side.
Their dream is a coin found under slanting

light, oblivion enough to damp down care
a while. But wish us all good health and reason
who wake sometimes, knowing we too have been
visited by importunate ghosts and have forgotten;

tell us what we dreamed, interpret for us the dream.

Garde de nuit

Dans nos villages suburbains, nos villes-dortoirs,
nous dormons en paix. Mais au coeur de la cité
sur les marches craquantes de cet abri humain
des gens passent qui pourraient être ministres

ou présidents our prêtres – mais ne le sont pas ;
avec des habits rayés de poussière et de gilets désassortis,
qui pourraient être fonctionnaires – mais ne le sont pas ;
gras et ridés et maladifs, ils hantent

nos rues, titubants, eux qui pourraient être
Platon, Luther, Hopkins, n'était une petite chose
qui dérapa et les fit dévier légèrement vers le côté.
Leur rêve. c'est une pièce de monnaie trouvée sous

une lumière oblique, assez d'oubli pour écarter leurs soucis
un moment. Mais souhaitez-nous à tous santé et raison
à nous qui parfois nous réveillons en sachant que nous avons
nous aussi reçu la visite de fantômes importuns et l'avons oublié ;

dites nous à quoi nous avons rêvé, interprétez pour nous le rêve.

Translated by Jacques Rancourt

Sibila Petlevski

Poet, novelist, playwright, performer, literary critic, editor and translator born in Zagreb, Croatia. Author of 20 books, member of L'Académie Mallarmé. Received the National Prize for Literature and Arts (1993) for her book of poetry *A Hundred Alexandrine Epigrams*. Founder and director of Literature Live International Festival in Zagreb. Nationally and internationally anthologized author. Writes in Croatian and in English.

Datumi Slave

Podizanje, razvijanje stjegova, spuštanje,
motanje i spremanje na rezervne položaje,
odakle će isti biti izvučeni na kalendarski
iste datume koji već sutra neće biti što su
bili. Datumi slave. Po jedan čovjek u svaki
pravokutnik prostrt u šareno. Poravnavanje
rubova. Prilaženje. Prilaženje spuštene glave.
Poravnavanje ukrasa. Udaljavanje. Napuštanje.

Stajanje podignutih podbradaka, podignutih
čela, gledanje uvis sklopljenih očiju svaki puta
nepogrešivo ravno u rupe koje su prosvirali
pucnji. Male, uredno poslagane eksplozije
časti. Kratka uznesenja. Uznesenja kratkog
dometa. Kamo god pogledaš izrešetano. I gore i
dolje i nebo i ljudi. Danas ćemo bajunetom izvršiti
pokolj zastava da nas sutra ne bi krpe nadživjele.

Dates of Fame

Raising, unfolding the flags, striking them,
folding them and putting them on reserve positions
where they will be pulled out on the same days
due to the calendar, which won't be what they used to be
as soon as tomorrow. The dates of fame. One man
laid down in many colours. Straightening of the edges.
Approaching. Approaching with head lowered down.
Straightening of the adornments. Moving away.

Abandoning. Standing with chins raised, raised
foreheads, looking high up with eyes closed every time
impeccably straight into the holes made with the bullets
that were put through. Little, neatly arranged explosions
of honour. Short ecstasy. Short term ecstasy. Wherever
you look, it is shot through. Up and down and sky
and people. Today we are going to slaughter the flags
with a bayonet, not to be survived by rags tomorrow.

Milan Richter

Richter has published 8 volumes of poetry and his selected poems appeared in several languages abroad, including French, Hebrew, German, Norwegian, and Spanish. Milan Richter has received the Swedish Academy's Translation Prize and the Golden Order of Merit for the Republic of Austria, as well as several awards and prizes in Slovakia. He served as vice-president of the Slovak PEN Centre and since 2005 he's been member of the Bjornstjerne Bjornson Academy in Norway.

Červom nevonia

Červ v elektronickom mikroskope sa hadí a hadí,
dáva za pravdu vedcovi: „Predĺžili sme mu život
o 40 percent." Hlas ustatý, oči červené.
„Zaplatí za to nezáujmom o párenie, nič mu
nebude voňať…"

„Život na Zemi vznikol iba raz. Červy tu boli
pred nami. Sme v príbuzenstve so všetkými tvormi."

Vieme....... Červy to vedia...... Už sa tešia
na svojich príbuzných...... Aj keby sme im
nemali voňať..... Aj keby sme im nepredĺžili život.
Pária sa, aby boli pripravené....... Aby tu boli.......
Aj vtedy, keď si požijeme dlhšie, než by sa patrilo......
Na slušných ľudí...... Ktorým život voni

Worms do not Smell It

The worm under the electron microscope is wrigling and wrigling.
It proves the scientist right. "We've lengthened its life
by 40 percent." A tired voice, red eyes.
"It'll pay for it by being uninterested in mating and
it will have no sense of smell."

"Life on Earth originated only once. The worms were here
before us. We are related to all creatures."

We know. The worms know this. They're already
looking forward to their relatives. Even if they can't
smell us. Even if we hadn't lengthened their lives.
They mate in order to be ready. To be here.
Even if we live longer than is decent.
For decent humans. Who can smell life.

Pýtal si sa jej...

... a že tě nesmím líbat a že s tebou nesmím spát...
Vladimír Holan (Ptala se tě...)

Sedel si s dievčinou pri bazéne
(na dolet motýľa od morského brehu),
čítal si poznove jej verše o priesvitných
bytostiach „medzi červami a vtákmi"
a spýtal sa jej mäkkých úst a temných očí:
„Ste ako prišpendlená babôčka jassius...
Prečo vo vašich básňach necítiť osudovosť?"

Chcela ti povedať: „Aj to, že si, je môj osud, že si...
ty, čo ma túžiš bozkávať a vyliať do mňa svoj žiaľ,
ty, čo netušíš, že v noci som zámotok a larva,
že po ránach vláčim doráňané krídla
blatom a kalužami nepreliatych sĺz,
pokým sa pod prudkým slnkom nepremením
na bytosť s medovým hlasom, s blúzkou,
pod ktorou spievajú nikým nehladkané ňadrá..."

Mlčala. Zdvihol si hlavu od jej veršov a videl iba
veľkého motýľa s čiernymi okami a pestrou blúzkou.
Oprel sa krídlom o dych tvojho desu
a vietor ho štuchal, zauškoval k moru,
k larvám a babôčkam a vtákom Orientu.
Spieval, ver mi, ten motýľ medovo spieval,
ale nikdy sa nedozvieš, o čom.

You Asked Her

> ... and because I can't kiss you nor sleep with you....
>
> Vladimír Holan (She asked you...)

You were sitting with a girl by the swimming pool
(a butterfly's flight away from the sea shore),
you'd once more read her poems about transparent
beings "between worms and birds"
and were asking her soft lips and dark eyes:
"You're like a Pasha butterfly on a pin.
Why don't I feel fatefulness in your poems?"

She wanted to tell you: "The fact that you are, that is my fate, that, too...
You who yearn to kiss me and pour your sorrow into me,
you who don't suspect that at night I'm a cocoon, a larva,
that until morning I drag my wounded wings
through mud and puddles of unshed tears
till under a fierce sun I turn into
a creature with a honeyed voice with a light blouse
under which sing breasts not fondled by anyone..."

She fell silent. You raised your head from her verses and only saw
a big butterfly with black eyes and a bright blouse.
It leaned its wing against the breath of your horror
and the wind caught it and slapped its towards the sea,
to the Orient's larvae, butterflies and birds.
It was singing, believe me, that butterfly, singing honey-sweet,
but you'll never learn what it was singing about.

Translated by Ewald Oser

Pat Boran

Pat Boran is a poet, fiction writer, publisher and radio broadcaster. He was born in Portlaoise in 1963 and currently lives in Dublin.

The recipient of the 1989 Patrick Kavanagh Award, he has published four collections of poetry, as well as *New and Selected Poems* (2005, reissued in 2007). Pat Boran received the Lawrence O'Shaughnessy Award for Poetry in 2008. He is a member of Aosdána.

The Drawer

The drawer is opened, by your hand.
What quest was this, has this become
just now in this unthinking gesture
of desire? The hand before you
alive with its own sense.

Phallus? Hardly. Sword? Perhaps.
But I was thinking something more
like guide or messenger whose news
is not in words and not in maps
but in the things themselves. Just look:

the pens, the clips, the torn-off stamps—
time tunnels, casual transports
to an elsewhere you had not intended
to explore, not now, not yet, yet now
if not the chosen then some promised land.

Jacques Ancet

Jacques Ancet est né à Lyon en 1942. Longtemps
professeur d'espagnol dans les classes préparatoires aux
grandes écoles littéraires et commerciales, il vit près
d'Annecy où il se consacre maintenant à son travail
d'écrivain et de traducteur. Il est l'auteur d'une trentaine
de livres (poèmes, proses, essais) Prix Nelly Sachs 1992,
prix Rhône-Alpes du Livre, 1994, bourse de traduction du
Prix Européen de Littérature Nathan Katz 2006.

Le Suspens, Le Cri

La beauté recommence. A chaque fois, c'est comme si elle m'ôtait les
mots de la bouche. Le ciel fume sur la montagne, l'eau scintille hors
de son nom. Dans la bouteille de celle qui boit brûle un infime soleil.
Petite nature, dit la voix. Tais-toi, répond l'autre. Le vent
ressemble à un visage.

— Qu'est-ce que tu cherches ?
— Ce que je trouve.

Les corps multiplient l'instant. Jeux d'ombre et de lumière.
Puis le soir vient dans les couleurs. Je suis perdu. Serait-ce la beauté ?

*

Les sandales sans les pieds, les pieds sans les sandales. L'ombre sans
la lumière, la lumière sans l'ombre. Les mots sans la bouche, la bouche
sans les mots. On pourrait croire que tout est réversible, mais rien
ne l'est. A chaque regard, tout recommence, s'achève. La chute du
tronc ou son ascension. Le ciel comme une lame. Le dossier,
le craquement. Au milieu, mes mains égarées, mon visage
que je n'ai jamais vu. Au milieu, ma présence, comme
une absence. Ou l'inverse. Au milieu, le suspens, le cri.

Jacques Ancet, *Chronique d'un égarement* (inédit)

Lyubomir Levchev

Lyubomir Levchev was born on April 27, 1935, in Troyan, Bulgaria. He has published over 20 volumes of poetry and two novels. Over 60 of his books have been published in 33 countries. He has been awarded the Gold Medal for Poetry of the French Academy and the title Knight of Poetry, the Grand Prize of the Alexander Pushkin Institute and the Sorbonne, and the World Award of Mystic Poetry Fernando Rielo.

He lives in Sofia. Levchev is the founder and editor of the international literary magazine *Orpheus*.

КЛЮЧ

Пиехме тихо,
когато чухме стъпките на сянката.
И аз станах да й отворя,
но тя се бе прехвърлила през оградата.
Тогава

Ловецът на проблясъци ми каза:
Виж какво,
я ми остави ключа под бърсалката.
Понеже се надявам да се върна пак,
понеже се надявам...
За разлика от Оня,
с когото сме си бърсали сълзите...
Остави ми ключа под бърсалката.
Както правят всички.

Вече не правят,
казах аз.
Но ще ти оставя ключа
под онзи облак.
Както правят всички мълнии.

А всъщност,
Господ не заключва.

La Clé

Nous buvons tout bas
quand nous avons entendu les pas de l'ombre.
Je me suis levé de lui ouvrir la porte,
mais elle avait déjà sauté le portail.
Alors

Le chasseur de fulgurances
m'a dit:
« - Écoute, laisse la clé sous le paillasson
parce que j'espère de revenir un jour,
parce que j'espère… »
Nous, pas comme « Lui »,
avec lequel nous avons essuyé nos larmes.
Laisse la clé sous le paillasson.
comme tout le monde.
« - Personne ne le fait plus » (ai-je dit!)
Mais je vais te laisser la clé
sous ce nuage
comme le font tous les éclairs.

En effet,
Dieu ne ferme jamais à clé.

ЛЮБОВ ВЪВ ВОЕННАТА БОЛНИЦА

Шинелът на нощта ми е голям
ще ни покрие двамата и ще се влачи по земята.
Ще заличи следите ни и ще останат само нашите слова
да странстват и понякога да се намират.

С оръжията съм си взимал сбогом
и то така, че Бог
ще ме запомни.
Но никога не съм бил в никаква военна болница.

Край тихия отровен Дон
съм се търкалял,
съсечен от клепачи на казачки.
Но никога не съм бил в никаква военна болница.

Между звезди и пясъци, и чума
с ужасния художник Гро
съм съзерцавал посещението на великите миражи.
Но никога...
И все пак вчера
ний бяхме с тебе в лазарета.

Покрити от шинела
като локва
сред локви от съсирена и още непролята кръв.
Сред купчини от гнойни бинтове и марли, и вериги "хеви
метъл"
лежахме ний прегърнати, не, вкопчени един във друг.

Ти бе запушила с целувка смъртоносната ми рана
и моята душа изтичаше
не в хаоса и в непрогледността,
а в тебе, светла моя пропаст.

На дъното. Там исках да се скрия.
Треперехме и двамата.
А покрай нас крещяха слепи, ампутирани, дрогирани,
обречени...
Повръщаха предсмъртен писък:
"Allons enfants! Allons enfants!"
"Egalite!", "Fraternite!"
Матросът със отрязани нозе
запяваше с последно вдъхновение:
"На крак, о парии презрени!".
"Rot Front!" издигаше юмрук безръкият.
"Avanti popolo!"
" No pasaran!"
"За Сталина, за Родину!",
"За Сталина, за Родину!",
"За Сталина!"
крещеше наказателният взвод,
а също и онези, Другите,
почти засипаните в гроба тридесетмилионен.
"Patria o muerte!"
"Venceremos!"

А може би и аз съм вече сляп.
И затова те галя като луд.
Чета те като брайлово писмо. "Прости ми!"
А ти ми шепнеш: "Не това! Кажи ми другото!
Кажи ми го отново!"
И аз крещя "Обичам те!" като осъден.
Тъй както се крещи последна дума.

Бъди спокойна, няма да ни чуят в лазарета двайстовечен
сред всички тези крясъци, стенания, проклятия, хриптене
и останало мълчание.

Когато дойдат утре сутринта гробарите за мен,
проговори отново и кажи, че вече си ме изгорила.
Кажи, че тъй съм пожелал, да бъда изгорен отделно.
Не казвай, че за твоя огън става дума.
А името ми може да стои при Другите на братската могила...
Но и това е много.
По-добре твърди докрая,
че аз не съм бил никога и в никаква военна болница.

Love in the Military Hospital

Night's greatcoat is large for us –
It will cover us both and still trail on the ground.
It will cover our tracks and just
our words will remain

to wander about and find each other sometimes.

It so happens I've bid farewell to arms,
yet in such a way that God
will remember me.
But I have never been in any military hospital.

By the quiet poisonous Don
I have rolled
sabered by Cossack girls' eyelashes.
But I have never been in any military hospital.

Among stars and sand and plague
with the dreadful artist Gro
I have contemplated the visit of the great mirages.
But I have never…
Yet, yesterday
we were in the military infirmary.
Covered by the greatcoat –
like a puddle
among puddles of clotted and not-yet-shed blood.
Among piles of pus-stained bandages and gauze
and Heavy Metal chains
we lay embraced, no,
clung to one another.

You had stopped my fatal wound with a kiss
and my soul was flowing out

not into chaos and the pitch dark
but into you, my light abyss.

At the bottom. That's where I wished to hide myself.
We were trembling, both of us.
While around us were screaming the blind, the amputated,
the drugged, the doomed...
they were vomiting death screams:
"Allons enfants! Allons enfants!"
"Egalité!" "Fraternité!"
The sailor with the cut-off legs
broke into a song with his last inspiration:
"Rot Front!"- the armless raised his arms.
"Avanti populo!"
"¡No Pasarán!
"Za Stalina, za Rodinu!"
"Za Stalina...!"-
the punitive squad was shouting,
as well as those - the Other Ones,
the almost buried in the thirty-million-graves ones.
"¡Patria o muerte!"
"¡Venceremos!"

And maybe I am also blind already.
And that's why I am caressing you like mad.
I read you like Braille: "Forgive me!"
And you whisper: "Not that! Say that other thing!
Say it to me again!"
And I shout: "I love you!" like someone just convicted.
The way one cries out his last word.

Don't worry, they won't hear us
in the twentieth-century military infirmary

among all these screams, moans,
curses, wheezes,
and residual silence.

When tomorrow morning the gravediggers come for me,
speak up again and say you've already burned me.
Say that's what I wanted - to be burned separately.
Don't say that you mean your fire.
As for my name, it may stay with the Other Ones
in the common grave...
But even that's too much.
Better claim until the end
that I have never been in any military hospital.

Anise Koltz

Anise Koltz was born in 1928 in Luxembourg-Eich. She is the founder and organiser of the international writers' festival in Mondorf, Luxembourg: 'Journées de Mondorf': and is now honorary president of this festival. She is a member of the Mallarmé Academy, of the Belgian PEN-Club and of the Institut Grand-Ducal des Arts et des Lettres. She lives in Luxembourg, has published many collections of her poetry and is the current honorary president of the European Academy of Poetry.

A la fenêtre

La lune pleine
recouvre les mendiants
de sa lumière emrpuntée

Tandis que l'odeur du sang
court les rues
une femme suspend
son hymen à la fenêtre
pour le faire sécher

Les étoiles

Le ciel est devenu
un abîme de clarté

Toutes les étoiles
des juifs gazés
sont épinglées au firmament

Le corbillard

Mes souliers
sont troués

Mes béquilles
souillées de boue

Je regarde passer le corbillard
qui emporte
tout ce que je n'ai pas vécu.

At the Window

The full moon
bathes the beggars
in its borrowed light

While the odour of blood
runs through the streets
a woman is hanging
her hymen at the window
to let it dry.

The Stars

The sky has become
an abyss of brightness

All the stars
of Jews who have been gassed
are pinned against the firmament

The Hearse

My shoes
are ruined

My crutches
soiled with mud

I watch the hearse pass by
that is carrying away
everything I never lived.

Sous le lit

Je serai seule
à mourir
avec sous le lit
mes souliers déroutés

Je t'aime

Je t'aime
parce que dans ta poitrine
résonne le bruit de la vie

Je t'aime
parce que ton amour
inventé pour voler
est un faucon
que s'est posé sur mon poing

Under the Bed

I will be alone
in my dying
with my aimless shoes
under the bed

I Love You

I love you
because the sounds of living
resonate in your breast

I love you
because your love
invented to fly
is a falcon
alighting on my wrist

Translated by John F. Deane

Alexandre Voisard

Born in Porrentruy, Switzerland in 1930, he was one of
the "poètes de la Libération" whose poetry, particularly the
legendary poems of *Liberté à l'aube*, marked the march of
the Jura towards the independence of an autonomous Swiss
canton. After several occupations he was elected "délégué
aux affaires culturelles" of his region. Today he lives in
France, close to his native country and has published a
great number of collections of his verse and prose.

Au bout du monde
sont les illusions
au bout de ton chemin
sont les espérances
Entre les deux il y a
le clair-obscur des sentiments
et le désarroi
de l'aiguille magnétique.

Où vais-je poète gravant
des mots au dos des lunes
où me porte
ce pas de nuage
appris hors des livres

nul ne sait
mais que ce soit à une soeur
imaginaire éternellement présente
nécessairement lumineuse
sur la page volante.

Tu as voulu voir le monde
tu voyages seul

dans les tunnels
tu fermes tes paupières
et tu vois plus clair en toi
qu'avec les yeux ouverts

les tunnels t'enferment
en leurs ténèbres
tu leur dis

"merci de me réconcilier
avec moi-même"

puis on s'oublie tout à fait
c'est comme si
on mourait vivant.

At the world's end
are the illusions
at the end of your road
are the hopes
Between the two there is
the chiaroscuro of emotions
and the disarray
of the magnetic needle

Where am I poet heading carving
words on the back of moons
where is this cloud-footstep
learned apart from books
bringing me to

nobody knows
unless it be towards an imaginary
sister eternally there
necessarily a source of light
on the flying page.

You wanted to see the world
you are travelling alone

while in tunnels
you close your eyelids ˙
and see more clearly within yourself
that when your eyes are open

the tunnels lock you in
to their darknesses
you say to them "thanks

for reconciling me
with myself"

then one forgets oneself completely
and it's just as if
still alive one were dying.

Translated by John F. Deane

Özdemir Ince

Őzdemir Ince, born 1936, is a poet, an essayist and a journalist. He has published several collections of his poetry and been translated into many languages. He has also translated several poets into Turkish, including Adonis, Alain Bosquet, Rimbaud and Cavafis. He has won the Max Jacobs prize for poetry.

AĞUSTOS 1936

1.

Buhurdanlıktan tüten bronz ağustos
mor damarlı incir sütünü damlat
trahomlu gözlerime, yaksın.

Görebileyim nasıl bir yağmur ormanı.

Göğsümü okşa, sırtımı kaşı, mısır yapraklarınla,
dinlesin sözümü yutağımdaki örümcek,
başladığım menzil son durak olsun.

Ağustos ! Benim olacak hayaletim

2.

Kaplumbağanın zırhı içindeyim
doğuştan kör gözlerim
killi toprak yiyorum acıkınca

baldıran çiğniyorum
susadığım zaman.

Peşimi bırakmıyor bir karınca sürüsü.

Düşünüyorum
ama hiçbir dilim yok.

3.

Zaman daraldı
uyanıyorum Küçük Gelin'in karnında,
birkaç saniye süren uyanıklık

ilk kez duyduğum bir aydınlık,
su sesi, suyun doğal sesi, doğada,

bir başka aydınlık daha var :
ceviz dallarının çağıldaması rüzgârda.

Kuşkusuz, bunlar,
Yetmiş yıl sonra bulduğum tanımlamalar

kum saatinin inceldiği yerde.

AOÛT 1936

1.

Que le bronze d'août, fumant de l'encensoir
verse dans mes yeux malades
le lait de la figue aux veines mauves,
Qu'il les soigne.

Que je puisse voir à quoi ressemble une forêt de pluie.

Caresse ma poitrine, gratte mon dos avec des feuilles de maïs,
que l'araignée dans mon gosier écoute ma parole,
que ce soit l'arrêt dernier du parcours entrepris.

Août! Mon fantôme prochain!

2.

Je suis dans la carapace de tortue
j'ai les yeux aveugles de naissance
de faim, je mange une terre argileuse

je mâche de la ciguë
quand j'ai soif.

un troupeau de fourmis est constamment attaché à mes pas.

Je pense
sans possèder aucune langue

3.

Le temps a rétréci
Dans le ventre de la mariée je m'éveille,
un réveil de quelques secondes

une clarté sentie pour la première fois,
le bruit de l'eau, dans la nature, le bruit naturel de l'eau,

il y a une clarté autre en plus:
le bruissement des branches de noyer dans le vent.

Elles sont sans soupçon, elles,
Mes définitions trouvées soixante dix-ans après

au lieu où s'amincit le sablier.

Traduit du turc par Claire Lajus

IRISH POETRY

A selection of work from some of
Ireland's contemporary poets

Thomas Kinsella

Thomas Kinsella was born in Dublin in 1928. He attended
University College, Dublin, entering the Civil Service,
before becoming a full-time writer and teacher in the
United States. He is the author of over thirty collections
of poetry, and has translated extensively from the Irish,
notably the great epic The Tain. He was a director of the
Dolmen Press and Cuala Press, Dublin, and in 1972
founded Peppercanister Press for the publication of
sequencs and long occasional poems. The editor of *The
New Oxford Book of Irish Verse* and of Austin Clarke's
Selected Poems and *Collected Poems*, Thomas Kisnella
is also the author of *The Dual Tradition* (Carcanet), a
critical essay on poetry and politics in Ireland. His awards
and honours include Guggenheim Fellowships, the Denis
Devlin Memorial Award, the Irish Arts Council Triennial
Book Award and honorary doctorates from the University
of Turin and the National University of Ireland. In 2007
Thomas Kinsella was awarded the Freedom of the City of
Dublin. Carcanet publish several of his books including
The Dual Tradition and *Collected Poems*.

'Kinsella is by now the most formidable presence in Irish
poetry'- Seamus Deane, *A Short History of Irish Literature*

'Kinsella's is a distinct, authoritative, critical voice, but
while his body of work might at times appear fragmentary,
even the fragments radiate' - Pat Boran, *Sunday Tribune*

The Last Round: an allegory

I

We were howling down off our benches
at the two figures leaning on each other's bodies,
remote and bare under the lights.

*

All their skills perfected for this meeting,
so that one might defeat the other.

II

It is a long while since they were first heard of;
since the scouts were sent out to confirm the rumours,
and the first serious offers were made.

They were confined immediately, each separate,
far apart; trained by specialists
and strengthened in bodily endurance.

Then their names were made public for the first time,
and the first contests arranged
– unimportant in themselves, but essential
for the experience, and as a first step.

One was sent out to meet a local champion
on his own ground; and floored him,
featuring with startled comment in the local paper.

After a like shock, the other came home
to great acclaim, and the sponsoring of local events.

III

The bell beat,
and echoed up into the dark spaces around us.
It was over.

The two bodies leaned on each other,
intimate under the lights.
Their fists hung loose in their leather,
their organs damp in their bags.

They were separated.
The arm of one was lifted up.
He was led back into the corner
and sat staring up at the dark,

where the business of the evening
was being completed between the main parties.

And she said:

There is an inadequacy
and an imbalance in the source material.
This is the basis of energy.

And there is a disrhythmia in some among you
– the watchful and the partly fulfilled –
a worrying for any evidence of purpose.

This gives no pleasure, except in relief.
But welcome it if it is offered. Use it
to the full. Trusting there will be

an easing of the disorder at a time to come.
But resigned. . .

She turned away, her voice tired.

...if there is not.

Chris Agee

Born in 1956 in San Francisco and grew up in New York, Massachusetts and Rhode Island. Since 1979 he has lived in Ireland. His poetry collections include *In the New Hampshire Woods* (The Dedalus Press, 1992); and *First Light* (The Dedalus Press, 2003). He has edited *Scar on the Stone: Contemporary Poetry from Bosnia* (Bloodaxe Books, 1998, a Poetry Book Society Recommendation); and *Unfinished Ireland: Essays on Hubert Butler* (Irish Pages, 2003).

He edits *Irish Pages*, and his latest collection, from Salt, is *Next to Nothing* (2009). He lives in Belfast.

The following poems are from Chris Agee's newest volume of poetry, *"Next to Nothing"* published in 2009 by Salt.

In Prvo Selo

In the tradition of the place, once or more a summer,
We return to our evergreen Žrnovo door
And find hung, leant or left round the bronzed handle
Or smoothed limestone threshold, some ghost-token
Of a visitor – a bow of straw, or sheer headscarf,
Or terrace cushion, or wildflower or bough plucked
Nearby at a moment's notice. Sometimes, too, a gift
Materializes. Some tomatoes perhaps, or grappa
In a second-hand bottle, maybe a book or compote,
Lavender and oregano out of the adjacent fields,
Small cakes from a neighbour's kitchen. And if
Merely a folded piece of paper, always with neither
Name nor note. Thus out of this village silence
Immemorial as Anonymous, you come to realise
You're expected to intuit whoever it might have been
Who wished or needed seeing you at the dog day's
Missed periphery. Though once in a blue moon too,
The gift-giver or visit, like a ghost guested all summer,
Asked after, stays unknown despite the guesswork.

In Prvo Selo

Naar plaatselijke traditie komen we zo nu en dan 's zomers
Terug bij onze met klimop begroeide deur in Žrnovo
En vinden dan aan, tegen of om de bronsbruine deurknop
Of de gepolijste kalkstenen dorpel een onverwacht teken
Van een bezoeker – een strik van stro, een dunne hoofddoek,
Of een stoelkussen, een wilde bloem of tak net
Geplukt in de omgeving. Soms is het ook zomaar
Een geschenk. Een paar tomaten wellicht, of grappa
In een tweedehands fles, ook wel een boek of compote,
Lavendel en oregano van de velden in de buurt,
Kleine koekjes uit de keuken van een buur. En al is het
Slechts een opgevouwen papiertje, dan altijd zonder
Naam of bericht. Zo leer je langzaam van deze
Oeroude en Anonieme dorpsstilte dat men verwacht
Dat je aanvoelt wie er geweest is, wie je kwam opzoeken
Of je nodig had aan de vage rand van de warme dag.
Hoewel een enkele keer de schenker of bezoeker
Waar je naar zoekt, als een spookgast die je de hele zomer
Onderdak hebt gegeven, onbekend blijft ondanks al je gissen.

Next to Nothing

According to the Sufis, suffering is a special sign
Of divine favour: so a new friend's letter

Tells me, verifying (almost) its theme of a new life
In the spirit of death. Once again, I hardly know

What to make of such an extraordinary gloss:
Which reminds me, like all the rest, of the human

Barnacled to the great right whale of Heidegger's Being,
Touching it has no idea what osmosis: or rounded,

Uncovered stones like Jesus's writing on the sand
At the vast strand at Macheraroarty. Everyone arrives

Into the cloud of my real unknowing, hoping
To make good the camp ruination

Of the small Taj Mahal of Miriam's life,
The Mogul invader of memory's love; even so, truth

To tell, there is strange comfort in the sage
Belief of others, like Rusmir's in Sarajevo,

A stone's throw from the market stalls ghosted
With the Second Law of Thermodynamics: suspected Sufi

Who has never written. Knowing myself nothing;
Nothing sure; or next-to-nothing. That is all.

January 2002

Harry Clifton

Harry Clifton, born 1952 in Dublin but has lived in Africa
and Asia, as well as more recently in continental Europe.
He has published five collections of poems in Ireland and
the United Kingdom, including *The Liberal Cage* (1988)
and *The Desert Route: Selected Poems 1973–1988* (1992).
Wake Forest University Press published his newest
volume, *Secular Eden: Paris Notebooks 1994-2004*, in
2007, which won the 2008 The Irish Times Poetry Now
Award. His poems have been translated into several
European languages, and *Le Canto d'Ulysse*, his selected
poems in French, was published in 1996. He teaches at
University College Dublin and is a member of Aosdána.

Crossing Sweden

1

Cold interior, older than history.
Time, you might say,
Arrested, on the eighth day

Of Creation – the silences of churches,
The bibles shut forever.
After Apocalypse, pine and birch

Eternally on the move
To claim it back, an earth betrayed
By Lutheran spires, hipped roofs.

Eros the love-child frozen out –
A shaggy horse by the water-butt
Eating its heart out, stamping its hooves. . .

Grant me a death-wish. Drop me here
To rot in the provinces. Spare me the train
Through Sweden and the years.

2

'. . .Hallsberg, my friend, as the nothing name suggests,
Is a place of transit. Here, the traveller waits
Between trains, and the assembled ghosts

A million strong, a hundred years old,
Thread themselves through the needle's eye
Of New World passage – souls, to be bought and sold

In the cornfields of Iowa, the studios of Burbank,
London's slums, the deepsea ooze
Off Greenland, where the blind Titanic sank. . .

An airbridge of glass is hovering over the lines
And the frostbound trains are still.
Do you hesitate forever, diseased in will,

As the miracle happens? They are passing through
To Canada, Argentina, the chances of a lifetime,
As you, my friend, must do. . .'

3

Insistently, a foreign tongue
I can only interpret as Song
Comes over the air, as the train roars on.

Even as it speaks
Ice breaks, and fast-flowing rivers
Take over, the dazzle of lakes,

The shutter-speed of sun through trees
As the mind clicks into gear
And the eyes unfreeze.

A windfarm's slow propeller
Threshes cloudky skies –
I wonder who lives out there, who dies,

And see my own reflection
Rushing past, to the greater world
Of Stockholm Central, Gothenburg,

As the changes are announced
In that Scandinavian, singsong tone
I recognise, now, as my own.

It wants to be helpful, to be kind.
Abroad in the north country
Of my own mind,

I hear it – any tongue will do –
Interpreting the hinterland,
Hurtling me through.

Eva Bourke

Eva was born in Germany and has lived in Galway. Among her poetry collections are *Gonella* (1985), with drawings by Jay Murphy, *Litany for the Pig* (1989), *Spring in Henry Street* (1996) and *Travels with Gandolpho* (2000), the latter two titles published by Dedalus.

A teacher and translator, she is also the editor of a major dual language English / German anthology of Irish poetry entitled *In Green Ink / Mit Gruner Tinte* (1996) and her other translations include an English language verison of Elisabeth Borchers' *Winter on White Paper* (2002). She has received a number of awards and bursaries from the Arts Council. Her latest collection of poems, entitled *The Latitude of Naples*, was published in April 2005.

Gardens

Early morning. Someone's playing Scarlatti sonatas
in the house that lies in a granite garden
by the sea. The notes walk single file on air
waves and high wires strung between roofs,
a well-tempered procession.
Is it any wonder that within minutes
blackbirds and larks called by to exchange tunes?

***

Later I went out thinking how for your entire life
you can carry the memory of a green garden
in your head or the memory
of a damnation in jade and blue mosaics,
and not know which is which.

***

Come down to the strand, the encounter
of sea and rock where all ideas are twofold.
Borderland. The idea of stone and the idea
of water. Two pebbles plus two runlets make
one world. Look at us, say the boulders, we shine,
we glimmer, we are splendid imprinted with the orange,
white and black macula of lichen, the pale green
lichen that prickles under your soles.
Clusters of sea pinks grow from hairline
cracks on us. A mystery.They raise their tufted heads
trembling and bending to the wind.
Come into our garden and rest - we are washed
clean and silent. What more could you wish for?

***

Heavy in my pocket the stones knock
against my side at every step:
Lie low when the high tides come.

***

The last judgement in the golden-walled basilica on the island
is made of small pieces of glass tinted with the ink of moth wings,
of buttercups, matted hair, bone splinters, blue glass, owl feathers,
coal, sugar, pewter, bitumen, jelly fish, finger tips, gold leaf, mussel
shells, bat droppings, metal, umbilical blood, chinese ink, fog,,
black silk, haemoglobin, eel skin, touchstones, cuckoo flower
petals, glacial snow, saliva, sea water, granite and quartz.

***

At low tide the boats lying on Moyrus strand -
how empty they are now, exposed
to surveillance from above - the sun's scorching lens or
anything else winged, beaked and on the cruise for
morsels or rare salt grotesques,

and how still they are now where all was movement,
gesture, lilt and drift.

They have sunk so deep into pale wet sand
their names can't be read. Were it not
for mooring ropes and the anchor
hooked to the rocks, we all might slip fast
from this measured and rooted world.

Swim or sink! The sea reiterates its old
imperatives tugging at a portal in its depth
to let the iridescent shoals flit
from dark exits.

Filled with light, the boats wait
in the morning's lit-up
auditorium where a herring gull stands
on a draughty rostrum lecturing
on the idea of flight.

We, too, wait to be lifted, for the wind
to leaf through
the next pages of our narratives,
to be called by name and returned to flux -
the luminous wild passageways.

Gärten

Früher Morgen. Jemand spielt Scarlattisonaten im Haus
in einem Garten aus Granit am Meer..
Die Noten wandern einzeln auf Schall-
wellen und elektrischen Leitungen entlang -
eine wohltemperierte Prozession.
Ist es ein Wunder, dass Amseln und Lerchen sofort
da sind, um Melodien zu tauschen?

***

Später ging ich hinaus und dachte wie man ein Leben
lang die Erinnerung an einen grünen Garten im Kopf
mit sich tragen kann oder die Erinnerung
an eine Verdammnis in jadegrauem und blauem Mosaik
und nicht wissen
was was ist.

***

Komm an den Strand, wo Meer und Felsen
sich treffen, wo alle Gedanken
zweifach sind. Grenzland. Die Idee von Stein und
die Idee von Wasser. Zwei Kiesel und zwei Rinnsale machen
eine Welt. Sieh uns an, sagen die Granitblöcke, wir glänzen
wir glitzern, wir sind herrlich bedruckt mit der orange-
weiß- und schwarzen Makulatur der Flechte, der blassgrünen
Flechte die unter deinen Fußsohlen prickelt.
Strandlichtnelken wachsen aus haarfeinen
Rissen auf uns. Ein Geheimnis. Sie heben
ihre zarten Köpfe, zittern und neigen sich im Wind.
Komm in unseren Garten, wir sind
gewaschen, rein und still. Was willst du mehr?

***

Schwer in meiner Tasche die Steine
schlagen bei jedem Schritt an meine Seite:
Bleib unten wenn die Flutwelle kommt.

***

Das jüngste Gericht in der goldenen Basilika auf der Insel
ist aus kleinen Stückchen Glas gefärbt mit der Tinte von
Nachtfalterflügeln, Butterblumen, verfilztem Haar, Knochensplittern,
Blauglas, Eulenfedern, Kohle, Zucker, Zinn, Erdpech, Quallen, Finger-
spitzen, Blattgold, Muschelschalen, Fledermauskot, Schwermetall,
Nabelschnurblut, chinesischer Tusche, Nebel, schwarzem Krepp,
Hämoglobin, Aalhaut, Prüfstein, Kuckucksnelkenblüten, Gletscher-
schnee, Speichel, Meerwasser, Granit und Quarz.

***

Die Boote bei Ebbe auf dem Strand von Moyrus -
wie leer sie jetzt sind, der Überwachung von oben
ausgeliefert, dem Brennglas der Sonne oder
allem, was Schnäbel hat, herumkreist
auf Ausschau nach Delikatem oder
seltenen Salzgrotesken

und wie still, wo alles Bewegung war,
Geste, Schwingung und Treibenlassen.

Sie sind so tief im nassen Sand versunken
man kann ihre Namen nicht mehr
entziffern. Hingen
Taue und Anker nicht
an den Felsen fest, wie schnell

entglitten wir alle dieser ausgeloteten
und verwurzelten Welt.

Schwimm oder sink: das Meer wiederholt die alten
Imperative, öffnet tief in sich
ein Tor und entlässt
schillernde Schwärme
aus dunklen Gängen.

Lichterfüllt warten die Boote
im Festsaal, wo eine Lachmöwe
am zugigen Rednerpult steht und über
die Idee des Fluges referiert.

Auch wir warten, dass der Wind in
den nächsten Seiten unserer Erzählung
blättert, uns hebt,
mit Namen nennt und
der Flut zurückgibt -
den leuchtend wilden Passagen.

Translated by the Author

Pádraig J. Daly

Born in Dungarvan, Co. Waterford in 1943 and now working as an Augustinian priest in Dublin. He has published several collections of poetry, among them *The Last Dreamers: New & Selected Poems* (1999) and The Other Sea (2003), as well as his translations from the Italian of Edoardo Sanguineti, *Libretto* (1999) and Paolo Ruffilli, *Joy and Mourning* (reissued 2007). His latest collection of poems is *Clinging to the Myth* (2007) in which he refelects on grief and personal bereavement and uses the voices of 18th century Gaelic poetry to respond to the challenges of a post-Christian Ireland.

Virginal States

I

In this new land,
Where a million flowers bloom showily
And the fancy of a night
Leads blithely to the actions of love,

A virgin heart is an awkward thing,
Its hurts and longings unaccountable.

II

Love left behind in the wedding hall rejoicing,
I drive through lanes
Flamboyant with whitethorn and lady lace,
Nursing a vague, insistent hurt,

My skin yearning for touch,
My heart a snow keep
Above the passes of Summer.

III

There is no time any longer for preludes:
Descriptions of savage roots
Twisting iron rails out of shape,
Rain on black streets,
Gaunt elms.

I have but one theme:
My body – poor foolish body –
Calling, not for any human touch,
But for God;
And His dereliction of me.

Peter Sirr

Peter Sirr was born in Waterford in 1960 and now lives in Dublin where, until 2003, he was Director of the Irish Writers' Centre. He works as a freelance writer, editor and translator and was editor of *Poetry Ireland Review*.

The Gallery Press has published *Marginal Zones* (1984), *Talk, Talk* (1987) *Ways of Falling* (1991), *The Ledger of Fruitful Exchange* (1995), *Bring Everything* (2000). His new collection *Nonetheless* and his *Selected Poems 1982-2004* were published in 2004.

In the Beginning

First comes the idea, someone's dream
of a winding street, of streetlamps.
Then sticks, wattle, ships flaring in the sunset,
serious heads on the coinage. Flagons
of small beer, ginshops, a tax on windows, doors.
Light dapples the civic water, a gallows
ghosts the green. Somehow the cathedral
makes it, somehow the wolf tax is revoked.
The centuries relax, flare up, relax.
The pubs are heaving,
stags and hens, bright buses bear
the sleepless to the suburbs, the conspirators
go over the details of the plan again.
It looks good. Silken Thomas, Isolde's eyelids.
Where is the other side of the street?
Any minute now the bubble-wrapped
department stores, electoral wards, silent armies
of statues. Oh protect us. Someone is singing
The Foggy Dew, someone is looking out to sea.
No, it must always have been there,
eternal as water, endless as air, the mudflats
singing, the rivers on fire, the districts
ringing out their numbers and their names.

Versions of Brecht
by Peter Sirr

Reading the Paper while Making Tea
(Zeitungenlesen beim Theekochen)
(Gedichte 1941 -47)

Early in the morning I keep an eye
on the earth shattering plans
of popes and kings, bankers and oil barons.
With my other eye I watch
the saucepan with the tea-water,
how it clouds and bubbles and clears again
and pouring over the rim snuffs out the flame.

As Our Cities Lay in Ruins
(Als unsere Städte in Schutt lagen)

As our cities lay in ruins
ravaged by the butcher's war
weak, cold and hungry
we began to build them again.

Figures from a dark age
we filled iron carts with rubble
and dug out bricks with our bare hands
that our children might be free.

Then we cleared the debris from the schools
and made space for our children, and washed
all the old dirt from the knowledge
we gave them, so they could use it again.

Fernando's Table

There was the turkey, tacchino, squabbling, impatient,
terrifying the hens and the gatecrashing pigeons

but that wasn't it

There was the peacock, pavone, kingly
on the rooftop, in the branches, his tail dipped in grasses

but that wasn't it

There was the family of goats, bearded, serious;
there was the cat in the piazza; there were chestnuts, fires

not those either, though nearly

There was you in your sunglasses in the service station;
there was a necklace of beads; there were trees, avenues

and that was closer, but not exactly

There was a long white road, almost, almost,
there was a table outside with wine and bread,

there were oil and cheese, a dish of lentils, as close
as you like now, the sun on the table, all of us eating,

all of us there as the lizards scuttled and the peacock
flew over and whatever we said has vanished

but the sun is somehow still on the table, the book
turned over, the oil softening the bread

and that must have been it, or something like it

pane, olio, formaggio, sole

Fernando's table washed with October,
all of us sitting there as if forever.

Enda Wyley

Enda Wyley was born in Dublin in 1966. She has published three collections of poetry with the Dedalus Press: *Eating Baby Jesus* (1994), *Socrates in the Garden* (1998) and *Poems For Breakfast* (2004). She has twice been a winner in the British National Poetry Competition and was the inaugural recipient of The Vincent Buckley Poetry Prize. She has also received an M.A. in Creative Writing from Lancaster University. She has been widely anthologised, including in the Field Day Anthology of Irish Writing, Irish Women's Writing and Tradition, Vols. 4 & 5. In 1997 and 2001 she was awarded bursaries in Literature from the Arts Council of Ireland/An Chomhairle Ealaíon.

Little Heart

In your folds tonight
are strawberries
to wash away,
some knots of tuna
netted there
and up along
your neckline
sweet corn beads
that make
a precious chain.

In your head
the dog is barking
and the small wall clock
is gently ticking,
your tongue clicking
to its time.
Little heart
not yet hurt
beat on.

Piccolo cuore

Tra le tue pieghe stanotte
Ci sono fragole da lavar via,
alcuni nodi di tonno
preso nella rete
e su, lungo
la linea del tuo collo
grani di mais
che fanno
una catena preziosa.

Nella tua testa
il cane abbaia
e il piccolo orologio da muro
ticchetta gentile
con la tua lingua che schiocca
a tempo.
Piccolo cuore
non ancora ferito
continua a battere.

Translated by Maria Ficara

Night Guard

When I get home you are upstairs,
standing in the square
that is our landing, your huge book
a block of pale corn light
wedged between your fingers,
your eyes squinting in the gloom,
your mind so fixed on Borge's words
that you do not hear me there at all,
breathing close to the turn of the stair,
watching how it must be sometimes
when I am away from you and her.

It is late and you shoulder presses
into the frame of her bedroom door
as though holding it solidly in place,
your hip like a firm nail in its side.
One socked foot presses on the other
and I know you would easily
jump into action if needed
because you are her night guard.
Intense reader but alert to every breath,
each restless move, all her tiny cries,
those early fears that populate the dark.

She has curled herself into a drowsy ball,
her fists tight under her hot belly,
her bottom to the air, one side of her face
gone pink in the furious stream of sleep,
turned away from the day she's left behind
dishevelled, well-worn, like her tiny clothes
flung on the creaking wooden floor.
Up on her wall the clock's fairy dreams

on a bed of strawberries and from where I am
time can be heard ticking and tocking and then
becoming your brave heart beating just for her.

Strange things in Strange Places
for Janet Mullarney in Magione Tower, Umbria

Go up the tower steps and find
strange things in strange places -
your red dog, old devil, clawing
a space on a crocheted shawl
high over the first stone floor,
knee-high blue men standing
in a row, who welcome beasts
and birds on their shoulders –
their skulls knots of creatures
jutting out towards the magic sun
and battlements of Magione.

The head of another beast
sticks out from the side of a bell jar,
nudges us down and out to a still night.
We stand high over the red-roofed town,
the cypress trees and ridged brown land.
Our giant shadows flap from the light
of the tower to its top tiny window,
then they clamber back inside, leaving
our real selves, bereft of strange things,
stumbling down alleys to a meal
where the host will never come.

Gerard Smyth

Gerard Smyth was born in Dublin in 1951. He has been publishing poetry in literary journals in Ireland, Britain and North America since the late 1960s.

He is the author of six collections: *World Without End* (New Writers' Press, 1977); *Loss and Gain* (Raven Arts Press, 1981); *Painting the Pink Roses Black* (Dedalus Press, 1986); and *Daytime Sleep*er (Dedalus, 2002), which also appeared in a Romanian translation in 2003. *A New Tenancy*, was published in 2004 and his latest collection, *The Mirror Tent*, appeared in 2007.

A Different America

Angels in the architecture.
Diamonds on the soles of her shoes.
That's what the singer saw when he made

his American tunes.
Songs of a different America.
The horizons that Audubon scanned

for birds of the air, flowers of the land.
On all sides the many voices:
Whitman, Melville, Thomas Merton

in the solitude of his hermitage,
looking up at stars on the flag,
stars in the firmament.

And Frost's New England woods
with their groves of abundance.
The cities with their citadels and subways,

their heroes cast in bronze.
That's what the singer saw –
a different America, the one he turned

into vision-songs, folk-canticles
with the rhythm of calypso, boom-bang of jazz.
Songs to make us join the dance.

The Holly Wreath is Dead

The holly wreath is dead in the Christmas rubbish.
The old calendar has no more days to give us.
There is the usual percussion of car-locks opening, shutting.
The early riser left his house in the chill before the sun came out
to thaw the night-frost on the cars and the silver blades of grass.
On the path that must be followed, sons and daughters
dawdle to the back-beat of their iPod-tunes.
They have questions to ask about the murdered and the missing,
about the wars they see on the news
and sometimes too about the God of their religion.

No Infidels

The women of Jerusalem were out
fetching the Sabbath bread.
Our taxi-driver said he'd show us the King David Hotel,
before taking us up to the Garden of Gethsemane.

It was early in the morning, a day that commenced
with the scent of spices, with chilly temperatures.
At David's Citadel, at Damascus Gate,
at the ancient walls that gathered in too many tribes
for one place, we needed shade not from the sun
but from the religious fervours inundating us,
making us feel a sense of being in medias res.

Between peddlers of holy pictures
and sellers of essential oils
we moved along with the mobs: shrine to shrine,
sleepwalking the Way of the Cross,
climbing to the top of the Mount of Olives.
At the gate to the Temple the Arab boy blocking our entrance
smiled and said: No infidels.

ESSAYS

Vlada Urosevic

Vlada Urosevic was born in Skopje in 1934 and is one
of the most noteworthy of contemporary Macedonian
poets. He is the author of eight books of poetry, as well as
stories, novels, essays and travel books. He has translated
into Macedonian authors such as Baudelaire, Rimbaud,
Apollinaire, Breton, Bosquet and Philippe Jones. He is a
member of the Académie Mallarmé and of the Macedonian
Academy of Sciences and Arts. He has taught comparative
literature in the philology faculty of Skopje University.

René Char : le duvet d'oiseau sur la vitre

by Vlada Urosevic

Lire la poésie de René Char, c'est s'abandonner à un léger vertige. Devant nous est une surface oblique et le sens glisse, ne nous permettant pas de le saisir. C'est pourquoi, tandis que nous nous avançons à travers les contrées de cette poésie, nous perdons notre assurance quant à la précision de nos sens. Au lieu de nous conduire vers les solides données de l'existence matérielle des choses, ceux-ci nous mènent, sans que nous remarquions quand ce changement a commencé, vers une perception sensitive de l'immatériel.

Il s'agit, visiblement, d'une écriture secrète. A peine pensons-nous devoir l'instant suivant arriver à la véritable signification, voici que devant nous, au lieu de l'explication rationnelle, s'ouvre un nouveau piège. C'est pourquoi lire la poésie de Char, c'est comme errer à travers un clair et transparent labyrinthe, d'où la sortie semble s'apercevoir, mais où jamais l'on ne peut parvenir jusqu'à celle-ci.

Ici, les projections abstraites du temps et de l'espace sont rendues à l'aide des choses familières et connues; c'est comme si l'on vous expliquait le continuum temps-espace à l'aide de grains de sable – mais au lieu d'une solide vision, devant vous est, encore, un nouvel univers don't les brumes ne se laissent pas réduire à de clairs schémas.

Un des grands messages de cette poésie est que la langue est un moyen non seulement d'explication mais aussi d'interrogation énigmatique. Ce poète ne dévoile pas des vérités facilement accessibles – il montre que derrière ces vérités existent des abîmes qui nous attendent avec les mâchoires ouvertes de leurs questions.

Sans soute ce penchant à la destruction de l'image solide et rationnelle du monde rapproche-t-il René Char du surréalisme. Mais là aussi Char ne se laisse pas enfermer dans des schémas tout prêts et des règles de comportement dessinées d'avance. Il occupe dans le mouvement surréaliste une place à part, à distance importante des modèles et formules reconnaissables – disons, comme la peinture de Juan Miro appartient au surréalisme sans adopter la démarche de Chirico de représentation réaliste de l'irréel.

Dans la poésie de Char, vu du point de vue de la tradition de la poésie française, se croisent deux courants très importants (et dans une certaine mesure opposés): celui de Mallarmée dans l'image poétique duquel il y a toujours divergence entre l'objet réel et son ombre linguistique, et celui de Rimbaud, des "Illuminations", où les mots s'approprient librement des significations nouvelles et inattendues. Mais en l'occurrence la démarche de Char a ses traits spécifique qui lui assurent une place toute particulière dans l'image de la poésie française, mettant ce poète hors du cadre des classifications générales.

Depuis ses débuts même jusqu'à la fin, dans cette poésie tremble une clarté patriculière. Dans le surréalisme – qui est, généralement, tourné vers les sombres paysages de la Forêt Noire du romantisme allemand et du roman gothique anglais – René Char (avec Paul Eluard) introduit les clartés de la Méditerranée. Il existe chez lui une image claire, sereine dirai-je même, don't on peut dire qu'elle domine dans ses visions, que celles-ci se déroulent dans le monde extérieur ou dans les paysages intérieurs de contemplation en soi-même. Ce poète possède dans sa sensibilité une curiosité particulière pour les nuances des sensations, pour les petits détails de la vie de la nature, pour la familiarité avec les autres sortes d'existences dans le monde quotidien qui nous entoure. Mais il parvient en même temps, dans ce qu'il exprime comme expérience de ces contacts matériels, à dégager comme message final un enrichissement spirituel du plus haut niveau, comme fruit de l'entrée dans le domaine de la transcendance.

Dans le célèbre texte "La Bibliothèque est en feu", il dit que l'écriture lui vient "comme un duvet d'oiseau sur ma vitre". Mais, derrière le bruissement à peine audible de ce messager venu du monde matériel, le poète entend la voix des sphères de l'esprit où s'entremêlent sans fin les grands tourbillons des questions qui n'ont pas de réponses – excepté dans les vers de certains poètes.

For God's Sake, Do Something!
by Fiona Sampson

It was going to be easy: I would simply cherry-pick one hundred highlights from the *Poetry Review* archive. After all, a centenary anthology is essentially celebratory. It has a licence to echo the curatorial practice of great travelling exhibitions, like the 1970s' *The Treasures of Tutankhamun* or, more recently, *Treasures of the Winter Palace*. Presenting important pieces out of context isn't just Cook's-touring for the MP3 generation, I thought: it can also bring these things to an audience who don't have access to them in their original setting.

Very few libraries hold a complete archive of *Poetry Review*. The Poetry Society's own holdings are no longer quite complete: one can't help wondering how much this has to do with its own public access remit. The British Library holds a complete set, but other copyright libraries do not. The holdings of private collectors remain private.

Even with unlimited access, though, reading one hundred years of Poetry Review is a sizeable, and not always a particularly digestible, task. In part this is because there's simply so much of the magazine. It was originally published monthly, then from 1915 to 1951 bi-monthly —although in a format smaller than today's—and didn't become quarterly until 1952. In part, though, this indigestibility also comes from a peculiar unevenness of quality. When editorial control has been taken in-house, either through direct editing by the Chair of the Society (during the long reign of Galloway Kyle, from 1916–47) or a house editorial board (as under the Chairmanship of Thomas Moult, from 1952–62), the magazine ceases to be a literary review and becomes an organisational mouthpiece. Yet where it is edited by a serious poet or critic, whatever their orientation, it contributes to literary history, transcending passing institutional concerns to rehearse contemporary attitudes to poetry itself.

Sometimes fussy, by turn cantankerous and charming, the Review, read over its lifetime, emerges as a great British institutional Auntie: infuriating, fascinating and conscious of its responsibilities as what Michael Schmidt has called the "magazine of record." Its public role leads it to comment on everything from the appointments of Laureates and Professors of Poetry to the responsibilities of editors;[1] to publish literary memoirs of purely specialist interest as well as of literary celebrity;[2] as well as to print newly discovered posthumous work, whether by Scott or Sorley.

The *Review* was founded as *The Poetical Gazette* in 1909. Issue title pages carried the legend "First published as the Poetical Gazette, May, 1909" until the 1930s. It was, and has for a hundred years remained, published by the Poetry Society of Great Britain – originally the Poetry Recital Society – whose centenary it shares.

Early issues of the *Gazette* made it clear that this was a members' newsletter. In 1911, however, the Society invited the poet Harold Monro to co-publish – and edit – the magazine. Monro had been living in Italy and fretting over the state of British poetry when Maurice Hewlett told him, in what has become the magazine's Founding Myth, "If you feel like that, for God's sake go back to England and do something about it." Monro therefore countered the Society's offer with a proposal for "an independent monthly such as the Society required, which might prove of direct benefit to its members, though not its actual property". *Poetry Review* was launched (with the *Gazette* as a supplement) in January 1912. As Monro's introduction to the first issue, very much a manifesto, suggests, that year was to prove extraordinary and dynamic. Monro engaged the major literary talents of his day – the first issue alone included essays by Edmund Gosse, Ford Madox Hueffer, John Masefield and Ezra Pound – as well as supporting the young poets of the Georgian movement. When Ezra Pound introduced early work by William Carlos Williams, he commented in so doing that "Having said recently that no man now living in America writes anything that is of interest to the serious artist," nevertheless, "considering the tolerance accorded in England to such authors as Mr Noyes, Mr Abercrombie and Mr Figgis, I think there are a number of American works which might with safety be offered to the island market." This provoked a furious response from Rupert Brooke: "Lascelles Abercrombie [...] is a poet, alive, and that is more than can be said of most of us. [...] The "tolerance" one accords to [such writing] is the tolerance thirsty men give to wine, or flowers to sunlight."[3] It's certainly not easy to hear the grounds for trans-Atlantic complacency in the characteristic opening stanza of 'The Fool's Song', which hardly foreshadows the later Williams's "No ideas but in things":

> I tried to put a bird in a cage,
> O fool that I am!

> For the bird was truth.
> Sing merrily Truth; I tried to put
> Truth in a cage!

According to T.S.Eliot, Monro assumed:

[...] a role of importance and value during the period of several years up to 1914. He cared passionately though not always quite discriminatingly about poetry and was one of the few poets of whom it can be said that they cared more for poetry in general than for their own work. He not only helped in giving publicity to what have been called the 'Georgian Poets' but to the work of poets of a more advanced type. People like Pound, Flint, Aldington and the other 'Imagists' [....]Flint's chronicles and reviews of contemporary French poetry which were published in Monro's magazine did a great deal [...] to arose an interest in French poetry in this country [...] anyone whose poetry he liked was sure of his support."[4]

However, after just twelve months, in which "I practically sold myself to the Society [...] I consented to defray expenses for one year[5] [...]" Monro was ousted by the Poetry Society. At their suggestion, he had signed no formal contract, and their decision was only revealed to him when he saw its announcement in the proofs of the *Gazette*'s December issue. Not surprisingly, the rupture was permanent, and Monro appended to its announcement the news that he would instead found the quarterly *Poetry and Drama*. Nevertheless, plans for the subsequently-famous Poetry Bookshop at 35, Devonshire Street in London WC1—a lease Monro had signed in the *Review*'s name—continued.[6] The shop, which was originally intended to "sell [...] what we have recommended" in the *Review*'s pages, included office space for the magazine, and a hall in which, during 1912, '*Poetry Review* Lectures' were presented by, among others, T.E.Hulme and the Irish Republican Darrell Figgis.

In a move which continues to pose questions about intellectual copyright for editorial 'brands', the Poetry Society replaced Monro with Stephen Phillips: a kind of compromise candidate. Undoubtedly a literary editor, he was nevertheless sufficiently in tune with the Society's sensibilities to stay the course for three years. The magazine took shape accordingly. As well as publishing such poets as Laurence Binyon, John Redwood-Anderson and Irving Tree, Philips committed a substantial proportion of his war-time issues to verse by Forces personnel.

The literary knockabout of its first four years perfectly demonstrates the pitfalls of picking a *Review* 'Top Hundred'. The general reader might expect a gallery of famous names. But PR didn't, of course, necessarily publish their finest work. What to make, for example, of a somewhat indifferent, if sincere, poem on 'Ypres' by Arthur Conan Doyle? Historical quarrels, while eminently researchable, place other pieces in parentheses. While Aleister Crowley's version of 'Villon's Apology' is occasioned 'On Reading Stevenson's Essay', G.K.Chesterton's 'Ballade of Cheerful Boredom' tells us, among other things:

> Let Gallup gallop, bloody spurred,
> Till Bacon owns to *Peter Pan*;
> Let Archer "spell" till every word
> Looks like a curse from Hindustan;
> Let Robertson, pride of his clan,
> Abolish God – and Tacitus;
> Let Nordau – be a charlatan;
> But these things will not do for us.

… How very true. Meanwhile, the specialists might wish to find their own tastes particularly catered for: with more work from the *Review*'s radical American canon, for example, by Denise Levertov, Alice Notley, George Oppen, Muriel Rukeyser or eco-Beat Gary Snyder. And then there are the glaring omissions: Modernism seems (*pace* Pound) a million miles away from Brookes's poetic worlds.[7]

So this anthology represents not the most important British poetry of the last hundred years, but rather *what has been seen as* most important. *Poetry Review*'s back-list offers something more than a record of the century's writing. It records the *reception* of that writing—by a particular, characteristic and characterising, British readership. This is a history of that jockeying between poetries and their reception which is called a mainstream. *Poetry Review*'s position at the heart of British poetry makes it something of a litmus paper for changing tastes and attitudes. Yet there's a bifurcation at the heart of the magazine's identity. Although an independent literary publication, it has historically remained responsive to the needs of an organisation with a membership including hobby, or emerging, writers: a bit like curating Tate Modern with the Cheltenham Watercolour Society in mind. Its tastes, such as the early resistance to Modernism, can appear conservative in retrospect.

And yet, the *Review* charts how the Hardy-Thomas-Larkin succession, with its mastery of pastoral and elegy, continues to provide the tactful 'blue note' in British poetry. It's to this tradition that Britain's Favourite Poets — the Betjemans and Fanthorpes — so intelligently refer, and which today's English elegists (such as Alan Jenkins, Andrew Motion and to some extent John Fuller) sustain. Meanwhile, the demotic, narrative verse of Kipling or Chesterton arguably finds its posterity in the 'anecdotage' of some of the New Generation poets particularly advocated by the *Review* of the 1990s. As art forms tried to adapt themselves to an accelerating complexity of social experience, twentieth century culture was characterised by a split between increasing complexity on one hand, and increasingly deliberate 'accessibility' on the other. In this context, the *Review*'s own bifurcated identity makes it a unique mirror of British poetic taste — and practice.

Stephen Phillips was succeeded by Galloway Kyle, who was simultaneously the Chair of the Society. For three decades, until 1947, he built the Poetry Society into what claimed to be the largest in the world, with an editorial office in the US. During his editorship the *Review* masthead incorporated approval from the *Literary Digest*: "The leading poetry magazine of the world... of international eminence." Kyle engaged as his American editor Alice Hunt Bartlett, whose surveys of 'Dynamic of American Poetry' appeared from Volume 14 until her death in 1949. He also lead a series of initiatives concerned with the history of poetry, such as appeals for a Tennyson Memorial Room in Lincoln Library or to maintain Edgar Allen Poe's cottage in Fordham. However, he was less interested in developments in contemporary British verse. Under Kyle's editorship the magazine reviewed, but did not much publish, work by established poets; instead largely printing the work of members, aspirant writers and competition winners. It's arguable that this closer relationship between magazine and Society was what enabled publication to continue, despite paper shortages, through two world wars – or, as a glorious editorial circumlocution from PR 5:3 has it, "The dislocation of peaceful interests."[8]

Kyle was responsible for at least one conspicuous editorial strength. Among the historical essays, anti-Modernist polemic and accounts of Poetry Society dinners and branch meetings he published were a number of extended surveys of international poetry. Simos Menardos contributed a lengthy series on Greek verse; Cranmer-Byng wrote on Chinese poetry; Federico Olivero on poetics, Sturge Moore returned to the topic of verse-drama. There were also explorations of poetry from Japan and India which it would be easy to dismiss as reductively colonialist, since the actual verse was mediated in each case by a Western essayist, were it not that this was the approach the magazine adopted to *all* international writing.

The *Review* was ahead of its time in another way, too. Long before the 1960s, when poets like Ted Hughes were to advocate working with schoolchildren—even before the 1944 'Butler' Education Act, which opened up education to young people regardless of gender or class, and produced such exemplary arts educationalists as Robin Tanner or Richard Hoggart—the Review was pioneering the writing of poetry in schools. In 1914, George Ayles told readers 'How London School Boys Find Expression in Verse'[9] . Soon, children started entering the magazine's Premium Prize competitions. By the 1940s, Mary Holliday was arguing that "It has been recognised by Professor Cizek in Vienna that there is such a thing as Child Art as distinct from adult art. [...] this creative impulse is for them an essential means of self-expression: its results are not to be judged according to adult standards or conventional rules of merit. Children have been allowed for many years to indulge their creative desires in paint [...] Yet language is used before paint by most children."[10]

By the 1940s, a group of repeatedly-published poets had come to supply much of the journal's tenor. In Kyle's earliest years, he had included several Noh plays by the Japanese proto-Modernist Yone Noguchi. Later regulars included Phoebe Hesketh, Ruth Pitter, Henry Treece, Vernon Watkins and Laurence Whistler. The indefatigable Marie Stopes contributed poems and wrote on Lord Alfred Douglas. Reviews were produced by the editorial team, rather than commissioned from a field of critics and freelancers. The results were undeniably homogenous, but the issues from this time also read as suffocatingly over-determined.

All magazines have a house style, of course. Some—Harold Monro's *Poetry and Drama*, Ian Hamilton's *The Review* (1962–72) and its successor

The New Review (1974-9), or, today, Michael Schmidt's *PNReview* (founded 1973 as *Poetry Nation*) and *Agenda*, founded by William Cookson and Ezra Pound in 1959 – have as their very *raison d'etre* their founding editors' vision of what poetry is. Each delineates its own personal "for God's sake...do something!" To read the hundred years of *Poetry Review* is to trace lines of influence—and sometimes, succession—both creative and critical. To take an example almost at random: George Barker's 'Letter to the Corpse of Eliot' ends "I hear you. I hear / you. I hear you."; his nephew John Fairfax asks that we 'Listen' to the younger poets he in turn reviews; while in 1967 the critic John Lehmann returns us to Barker. Groups —almost movements—of poets periodically combine to articulate a new English- or Scottishness: Norman MacCaig's 1966 'Poetry in Scotland' feature is a bench-mark, and that nationhood is in turn refigured by Robert Crawford, W.N.Herbert, Kathleeen Jamie and others in the late 1990s. A couple of years earlier, it's fascinating to compare Sean O'Brien[11] and Don Paterson[12] as they each square up to the giant figure O'Brien calls 'The Totalizer', Ted Hughes. No less interesting is the 2001 review in which Peter Porter contextualises Sean O'Brien's work with his own earlier suggestion "that a new school of poetry was emerging which would take up the baton from Auden's Thirties generation and bring back intellectualism and populism [...]"[13]   It's as revealing to read E.A.Markham reviewing Stewart Brown's reception of Derek Walcott—tracing a line of intellectual succession—as it is to read Walcott himself.

At the same time, *PR*'s particular remit is to address no one clique or movement, but rather a national audience. It canon-forms by being often almost the sole contemporary source for many with an interest in poetry *and* by working with the best writing. Just as poets may write towards an Ideal Reader, so this audience is a *de facto* check and balance which helps the editor prevent the magazine from talking to itself, or to an in-crowd of initiates.

If Galloway Kyle's response to this readership was to make the magazine the mouthpiece of aspiring writers, one who developed rapidly under this policy was Muriel Spark. She made her first appearance in spring 1947 with the Premium Prize-winning poem, 'On Seeing the Picasso-Matisse Exhibition, London, December, 1945.'[14] Thereafter she became a regular contributor. She also started to review. Still, it must have been a surprise when she became Kyle's successor as Editor. Naturally, Spark understood the link between critical and creative practice. In an editorial on 'Criticism, Effect and Morals', she argues that the critic tends to compensate for his "anxiety" about contemporary verse by over-analysis, "as if he were to examine a tear-drop under a microscope in an endeavour to analyse grief."[15]

Spark also initiated the payment of fees for published work. At a stroke, this professionalized the *Review*. According to some accounts, it was also what caused Spark to be replaced by John Gawsworth in 1949. As her *alter ego* in *Loitering with Intent*, read as a *roman à clef* of her time at the *Review*, says, "The wages [...] offered were of 1936 vintage, and this was 1949, modern times. But I pushed up the starting price a little, and took the job for its promise of a totally new experience."[16] Her 1992 memoir, *Curriculum Vitae*, reports that Spark had to resign in order to be paid. The magazine was not to appoint another woman editor for over half a century.[17]

Gawsworth, who early acknowledged Monro as his "mentor", was, like Spark, a serious editor. Volumes 39–42 see the first appearances in the magazine of Dannie Abse, Frances Cornford, Lawrence Durrell, Robert Graves, John Heath-Stubbs, Vernon Scannell and, perhaps surprisingly, Hugh MacDiarmid. Gawsworth was succeeded by an editorial committee chaired by Thomas Moult. A decade later, in 1962, John Smith took over, and the magazine sprang back to life. In 1966, Smith was in turn succeeded by Derek Parker, who dropped the definite article from the *Review*'s title. This was a high middle period of British twentieth century poetry—then widely affected by The Movement and inflected by the BBC, where George Macbeth was in charge of poetry programming from 1955–76—and PR was publishing Jack Clemo, Veronica Forrest, Elizabeth Jennings, George MacBeth (alas, for this anthology, chiefly in a series of verse-novellas), Rosemary Tonks, and Jon Silkin, alongside critical writing by Robert Graecen, Philip Hobsbaum and David Holbrook.

As if to demonstrate that the 1970s were a transitional passage in British poetry, 1971 (Adrian Henri, Martin Booth, Anthony Rudolf and Eric Mottram) and 1978 (Edwin Brock, Harry Chambers, Douglas Dunn and Roger Garfitt) were years of guest editors. Each also identified a future editor. Under Mottram (1972-77), the *Review* was at the centre of the radical poetics of the Anglo-American "poetry revival". Mottram published Ginsberg, Levertov, Snyder, Ferlinghetti and Rukeyser. From 1975 to '77 he adopted an A4-format, whose cover doodles and internal typescript suggested the notebook work-in-progress shared among friends. However, his tenure also crystalized frictions which existed within the Society, and within British poetry, between radical and more organically tradition-led poetics.[18] In many ways, these frictions were more dangerous for the Review than those which had been played out between Modernism and its detractors. What had happened before the second world war had sometimes opposed literary writers and critics to the amateur writer and reader. Now, however, the profession itself was split between remarkably evenly-balanced forces: both of them represented among the *Review*'s contributors and readers and within the Poetry Society's staff and Board.

Strangely responding to a thirty-year cycle, this struggle for the control of the poetry mainstream has been echoed a third time in the final decade of the *Review*'s maiden century. The rise of performance poetry has largely excluded a second generation of poets drawing on oral traditions —the successors to figures like Linton Kwesi Johnson, Grace Nichols or Benjamin Zephaniah: particularly but not exclusively Black British young poets—from what it dismissively calls 'page poetry'. While the *Review* records this shift too, it must often do so by omissions and silences.

The savagery of the wars which marred Mottram's tenure wasn't repeated under the custodianship of Roger Garfitt, who inaugurated a succession of poet-editors in the 1980s. Garfitt was succeeded by Andrew Motion (1982–83), Mick Imlah (1984–86) and Peter Forbes, who came to the role as a poet but whose lengthy editorial tenure (1986–2002) defined not only the tastes of a poetic generation but to some extent his own professional identity. Motion and Imlah passed brilliantly through, on their way to becoming successive poetry editors at Chatto & Windus—and later, in Imlah's case, the *TLS*. With the discreet, firm hand of intelligence, each managed to publish the poets who mattered then and who still matter more than two decades on. They achieved this in slightly different ways. Motion was perhaps the shade more conservative force, commissioning surviving greats: he published Philip Larkin's notorious review of Sylvia Plath, 'Horror Poet', and commissioned 'A Birthday Tribute' for Larkin's sixtieth from Harold Pinter, Gavin Ewart, A.N.Wilson and others. Imlah was very much the bright young man, identifying certain ideas, such as Englishness – as well as writing by peers such as Alan Hollinghurst – as particularly interesting. His *Review* is gossipy, editorial and vigourous in its assumption of high standards. An article titled 'Woman Wins', for example, opens: "The National Poetry Society Competition has again (see last year) failed to unearth convincing winners from a total of 12,000 submissions."[19]

Under Peter Forbes, the *Review* experienced perhaps its greatest period of editorial transparency. This is not to say that it was more generous than usual to poetics which differed from editorial taste, but rather that it perfectly reflected a zeitgeist. The mid-eighties saw the Central European poetries which had first been advocated by Ted Hughes and Daniel Weissbort move into the British mainstream. *PR* published Miroslav Holub, repeatedly, alongside Jaan Kaplinski, Piotr Sommer and Nobel laureates Milosz and Szymborska. But the Forbes years are perhaps best characterised by 1994's *New Generation* promotion, based on the very successful *Granta Best of Young British Novelists* (1983, 1993, and indeed 2003). Of course, there are many more publishing resources, and readers, for fiction than for poetry. While the *New Gen* promotion, which was intended to resist "the last gasp of a system of patronage"[20], made the careers of the twenty baby-boomers it nominated, it also sucked necessary oxygen from the rest of British poetry. A generation of arts administrators and teachers of poetry growing up on the *Review* lost the wider sense of what else was going on, especially among older and younger poets.

Culturally, though, this was an interesting moment. Not only did it mark the ascendancy of league-tables and the arrival of sales-trump-all in poetry; it was also the first time that a generation or group emerged that was not driven by shared artistic agenda but constructed by external forces, in particular a narrative about "success". Not surprisingly, when Peter Forbes moved on, the *Review* experienced a rebound. From 2002–5, *PR* was steered in a rigorously anti-poetry-*lite*, dynamic and criticism-led direction by an academic, David Herd, and a member of the TLS editorial team, Robert Potts. Potts and Herd were interested in post-modernity, critical intelligence and intersections with sophisticated visual culture. They were unafraid of seriousness and risk, elements which were at enough of a premium for their editorial policies to be read, sometimes, as more uncompromising than they in fact were.

Since 2005, the magazine has attempted to reconcile dual responsibilities: to represent the whole range of good practice in the country, and to steer and shape the mainstream. To show what's going on and influence it at the same time may sound paradoxical; but responsive leadership—a bit like an elective democracy—makes of canon-formation something incremental, and organic, achieved through quarterly development rather than the hit-and-run intervention of an anthology. As an early Monro editorial 'Notes and Comments' says:

> We continue to hope, however, that the existence in England
> of a periodical organised, unlike any other English periodical,
> for the publication of only good poetry (when such is forthcom
> ing), regardless of subject or style, may act as a stimulus and an
> encouragement to English poets, both known and unknown.[21]

What will *Poetry Review* look like over its next century? It's difficult, and perhaps beside the point, to speculate.[22] As Pound said in an early issue, "To give sound criticism of man's work after it is published is so difficult a task that we find it rarely done well, but to criticise a man's work before it is written is a task so very difficult that even I hesitate before the undertaking."[23] Whatever shifts are taking place in British poetry at the moment—greater poetic diversity, the renaissance of the through-composed collection and verse-novel, neo-Romanticism and its engagement with the authentic, or spiritual—will be way-markers for the next five years at most. Editors are often asked what new talent they've "discovered". But, unlike the editor of a book-list, whose work is to nurture the individual development of particular poets, the magazine editor's task is not *primarily* to discover and nurture *individual* talent, but to support all fine poets in writing well at every stage in their career. Movements in poetry arise at particular cultural-historical moments, rather than continually. The editor's role is to help keep the whole field healthy and vibrant. The radical, disciplined attention a good editor employs includes the ability to concentrate that attention wherever it's needed: incidentally the best insurance that the next thing, whatever it will be, can emerge undistorted.

To read with this active sense of responsibility requires a strong sense of the reading self, that reflexive experience of consciousness and its agency which used to be called subjectivity. Editors are, after all, simply readers — albeit of a peculiarly committed kind. Whatever professional discipline they bring to bear, each has an *individual*'s perspective on what is influential, what over-rated, and what unmissable. To edit is to participate in the culture of the day. And so, thus, is to read.

1. For example, 'On the Reviewing of *The Poetry Review* 17, pp277–9; or Yevgeny Vinokurov's 'Poetry Editor' in PR92:1, pp5–6.
2. These include Ernest Hartley Coleridge's memoir of 'The Genesis of the Ancient Mariner' (*PR*2:1 pp11–15); Rosalind Wade's memoir of 'The Parton Street Poets' (*PR*54:4, pp290–7); Ruthven Todd's 'Memories of Normal Cameron' (*PR*76:1–2, pp95–7).
3. PR1:9, pp.519–20.
4. Marvin Magalaner, 'Harold Monro and "The Poetry Review"', PR40:5, pp.340-347.
5. Magalaner 1949 p.342
6. Devonshire Street, off Theobald's Road, has since been flattened and renamed Boswell Street.
7. Yet 'Prufrock' was to be published less than three years later — and, what's more, by Poetry, the *Review*'s American peer. Harold Monro: "We welcome with enthusiasm the foundation in Chicago of Poetry, a "Magazine of Verse, to be published for the encouragement of the art."" ('Notes and Comments', PR1:11* p423). Stephen Phillips: "Poetry, the Chicago magazine of verse which is in the happy position of being handsomely guaranteed and assured of a comparatively long life [...]" (PR3 [no issue numbers], p296)
8. So it is ironic that it was Monro who should have been accused of just this policy in a stinging review by The New Age: "Each month this Review belauds verse-writers whose achievements should have been kept as a private family joy." PR1:8 p1/353
9. Vol 3, 185–9
10. Mary Holliday, 'Verse-Writing in Schools' PR 36/7*, pp.225–9.
11. 'The Totalizer', 84:3, pp 58–9.
12. 'Strathspeys and Death Metal', 85:1, pp32–3
13. 'At the Helm' PR91:1, pp61–2
14. PR37: Apr–May, pp165–7.
15. 'Verse-Writing in Schools', PR39:1 p4 (pp3–6).
16. Muriel Spark, Loitering with Intent Virago Modern Classics, 2007, pp.4–5.
17. Although Tracy Warr co-edited Mick Imlah's first three issue.
18. Cf Peter Barry, Poetry Wars: British Poetry of the 1970s and the Battle of Earls Court (Salt, 2006).
19. PR 73:4, p37. The "woman" was Carol Ann Duffy.
20. According to Peter Forbes in *PR*84:1, pp4–6.
21. PR 1:9, p423
22. And questions about digital format are beside the point here: the Review will be published in whatever format texts are being published in.
23. PR 1:10, p481

'Poetry Europe / Europoésie' has a different editor for each issue, and is edited from one of the countries represented in the Academy. This first issue is edited by John F. Deane, from Ireland, and has a certain bias towards Ireland. The second issue will be edited by Vlada Urosevic of the Republic of Macedonia.

Material for the journal is commissioned by the editor. Unsolicited material must be accompanied by an International Reply Coupon, a self-addressed envelope, and a covering letter.

The Academy's website is: www.poetryeurope.com